NO MATTER HOW GOOD THE LIGHT IS

This is for Cheryl ...
who knows about saints
selecting colors —

Best wishes

Ed   '98

Books by EDWARD BOCCIA

Poetry

Moving the Still Life   (1993)

No Matter How Good the Light Is: Poems by a Painter   (1998)

NO MATTER HOW GOOD THE LIGHT IS

Poems by a Painter

EDWARD BOCCIA

TIME BEING BOOKS
POETRY IN SIGHT AND SOUND
St. Louis, Missouri

Time Being Books®
10411 Clayton Road
St. Louis, Missouri 63131

Time Being Books® is an imprint of Time Being Press®
St. Louis, Missouri

Time Being Press® is a 501(c)(3) not-for-profit corporation.

Time Being Books® volumes are printed on acid-free paper, and binding materials are chosen for strength and durability.

ISBN 1-56809-044-7 (Hardcover)
ISBN 1-56809-045-5 (Paperback)

Library of Congress Cataloging-in-Publication Data:

Boccia, Edward.
    No matter how good the light is : poems by a painter / Edward Boccia.
    — 1st ed.
        p.   cm.
        ISBN 1-56809-044-7 (alk. paper). — ISBN 1-56809-045-5 (pbk. : alk. paper)
        I. Title.
    PS3552.O273N6   1998
    811'.54—dc21   97-50548
                                                                        CIP

Cover art by Edward Boccia, *Self Portrait*. Courtesy of the artist.
Book design and typesetting by Sheri L. Vandermolen
Manufactured in the United States of America

First Edition, first printing (March 1998)

Acknowledgments

I wish to express my thanks to Professor David Clewell, of Webster University, for helping me with the formal aspects of my poetry. As for Dave's insightful remarks about art, life, and the power of the word, there aren't many who are his equal.

I am also deeply grateful to two very professional people: Jerry Call, Editor in Chief of Time Being Books, and Sheri Vandermolen, Managing Editor. These gifted editors not only enhanced the clarity of my work, they have given me a deep respect, if not a sense of awe, for what it takes to get it right.

Finally, I wish to thank these publications, in which the following poems previously appeared: *Live Poets Society* ("Walking in Circles") and *Orbis* ("Outlived by Seurat").

To Alice, Antonio, and Jennifer

CONTENTS

DISCOVERY

REFLECTIONS

THE BLIND ARTIST

NO MATTER HOW GOOD THE LIGHT IS

DISCOVERY

* This symbol is used to indicate that a stanza has been divided because of pagination.

From the Neck Up

When I was young
I read every book in the library.
Later, I devoured the entire
Encyclopaedia Britannica.
I didn't want to miss a thing.
By the time I was thirty-two
my head was so full of knowledge
it fell off,
rolled across the library floor
and out the door.
This took twenty years.
I don't remember how long
it rolled across the grass
before it stopped on a gold-
and-yellow leaf,
blinked its eyes, and whispered,
in the beginning was the word,
but in the end is
color.

First Things First

1

I'm painting a naked woman
asleep in a rowboat at sea.
Love has to dream before it wakes up.
I'm putting a live fish in the boat.
Love had gills before it had brains.
I place an anchor at the woman's feet,
sometimes at her head.
Either way, the anchor stands for God.
When I drop anchor with the prongs
stuck on the bottom, it's not because
God is dead. I just need a little more time
to get back to the woman,
to wake her up and have her look out
over the bow, to paint shiny highlights
on her hips, to lay the paint on thick
where the waves slap her belly.
A few last minutes to paint the woman's shadow,
extending beyond the boat,
a quivering passage full of blues.

2

Whenever I do a painting of a man standing
on a beach, looking down into a rowboat,
it means he's thinking of taking the boat out
on the roughest journey of his life.
When I paint two oars resting in their oarlocks,
the man knows it will take a lot of rowing
to convince the ocean he's no landlubber.
Sometimes I put him in the boat, way out at sea.
The wind is so strong and the ocean so choppy,
the man falls overboard.
As soon as I dab white paint on the water,
you can bet our traveler is drowning.
If you look real hard into the dark,
green color of the ocean, he's looking up,
trying to find the hull.
I would get him to kick and come to the surface,
but I can't save a man with just paint and turpentine.
*

I remember once he floated back up all by himself. That's when I got busy and rendered him facedown in the water, his arms stretched out like tentacles, the back of his skull bobbing like a melon.

She's in Love

Two strokes of paint,
and my canvas is alive with Adam and Eve.
A squiggle here and a dot there,
and I've got the serpent
sneaking up on a buttercup.
Watch how I brush in some pink,
the way I mix it with yellow;
it's 5 a.m. in the garden,
and the sun is about to come up.
Look at the way I render Adam,
his muscles bulging.
Look at Eve, rolling around in the pansies;
She's in love and doesn't know it.
Look at the purple shadows under her breasts;
Love has its grief. But it also has its joy,
like those streaks of green in her hair.

Deciding What to Paint

When I paint an apple,
Cézanne rolls around in my belly.
If I use little pink strokes,
Renoir sits up in my ear and shouts.
Tones bring on Goya as if he wants
to poke my eyes out. When I paint shadows,
Caravaggio draws his sword.
I could paint deep space
and put a cow in the background,
but I might turn into a bull,
or I could paint horses trotting
in a meadow, but then there are those horses
running in a circle, painted by Rosa Bonheur.
Maybe I'll paint a black dog running so fast
the black will drip a thousand legs,
or else I'll make a still life
that's so still the pears won't dare look
at the plums, the bread in the breadbasket
will refuse to nudge the wine bottle,
which will be too timid to talk to the napkin,
while the knife, sticking out over the edge
of the table, can't fall off,
what with the fork holding it down.

The Art Teacher

OK, he said, put a little yellow in it,
and then put some more yellow in it after that.
Pep it up, especially the right-hand corner.
Where are you going to put the sun?
How about the rays?
Will the moon still be out?
You want a picture trapped between
day and night, don't you?
Think about it.
Why use black when there aren't any shadows?
Is that spot of red a berry or blood?
Think of buttercups and azaleas.
Put mountains in the background.
Paint a guy on a horse in the valley.
Paint some bones and a cactus.
Include an elephant and a cheetah.
You want the picture to be the whole world,
don't you? For God's sake,
don't sign it there!

Drawing Without Color

George takes his pencil and makes a dot
on a piece of smooth, white paper.
He draws a line, as if it's growing
out of the dot — worm on its way.
The head of the worm wiggles 'round
full circle and touches its tail.

Now George has a circle without a tail.
After he fills in the circle with dot
after dot, he rubs a shadow round
the edges, till an eye stares from the paper.
With a few more lines, he draws a nose the way
Rembrandt did: light on one side, growing

dark on the other, and nothing growing
underneath except a curly mustache like the tail
on a pig. When George adds a beard, the way
he does it is by smearing a tone, with a dot
here and there for texture. The rest of the paper
is flat as space in a cubist picture, not round,

not even disturbed by a round
cloud or a living cherub. Nothing is growing
or flying in the corners of the paper
except where George sketches a tail,
then the body of Satan, with a dot
to mark the place for the tail, way

in back, at the bottom of the spine, the way
with all devils. George used to draw bright, round
apples years ago. As he was a pointillist, the dot
was everything, and like all young artists growing
into manhood, he couldn't draw a tail
on the back of his model; she was as pure as his paper

was white. George is old; his skin is like splotched paper.
His beard is gray and short, not long the way
it was on Walt Whitman, not made up of one tail
after the other squirming round,
like the beard forever growing
on Michelangelo's Moses. Today, George started with a dot.

Tomorrow he'll start with a tail and make it look round.
He'll put a dot in the sky for the sun, with rays growing
brighter and brighter, the way they always do on paper.

Walking in Circles

Do what I do: think of smoke
going up in squares, of light
coming down in cubes.
Imagine yourself in my shoes, walking
the way I walk, in circles,
with my head bowed.
Now consider this: the rug
under your feet has purpose
and the design in the rug
is a secret code. Do not
try to decipher that code;
do not try to guess what the colors mean.
Most of all, quit thinking red stands for blood,
forget about grief crying like purple.
Do what I do: lift your head
and look up,
swing your arms,
continue to walk in circles
but expand them,
and keep expanding them
till the circles swallow the whole room,
except the chairs and the little table
with the apple and the knife on it
and the letter you got yesterday
you won't ever open.

Seeing What Isn't

Eugene doesn't see the apples and the pears.
He doesn't see the platter
or the window,
the olive trees outside.
He does see space crawl between
the olive trees.
He sees it grow fingers,
which wrap themselves around each olive.
He watches space come in through
the window.
It grows feet and walks toward the apples
and hugs them.
It approaches the pears
and rubs them; then
it sits on Eugene's lap
like a child who needs love.
Eugene hugs space; he kisses it.
It smiles
and goes up in smoke.
When the air clears, Eugene sees
six apples
two pears
and a platter.
He stares at the olive trees outside.
They twist as if in pain.
Every olive is growing an eye.

A Look Inside the Brain

Bosch painted light
better than anybody. Who can ignore
those little fires he created
in his landscapes? The red logs,
the blue smoke, and the light of the fire
reflecting upon a tree, and the tree
going up in flames.
Or maybe Turner's light
is the most luminous.
Not a hot light but an explosion of yellows,
like a stormy sky at sea.
Because Cézanne's mind was a boat,
his light was in the hull. Maybe
that's why his apples don't burn
a hole through our eyes
like Monet's haystacks.
And nothing really cuts through a color
like Gentileschi's sword.
Nothing collects the intensity
of color like an El Greco halo.
Not one picture freezes the blood
as much as Picasso's *Guernica*,
and only the *Guernica* gets the blood boiling again.
Everything depends on how we kneel
before a painting. Everything in a painting
is connected to pieces of paint
in our bodies. All the lines
and tones in a painting come
from the lines and tones in the brain.
Open the skull, and there they are:
the tensions in the spaces between
form and content, and energy bending
like a painter over his palette.

Mixing Makes It So

When I mix yellow with green,
I think about the dandelion I picked
when I was twelve.
I see myself at fifteen, talking
to my brother, two kids in the cellar,
making plans — that happens when I squeeze out blue.
Red is blood, but not because it bleeds.
More red and some purple was me bleeding
to death last week.
Globs of white tell me I could live forever,
provided I don't paint with black.
So what I outline with black? I delineate
apples, berries, and roses, all with black.
Think of black and white mixed together.
Put some of that gray into some
of that yellow-green; add a stem.
Now you have a twelve-year-old kid
in the body of a seventy-year-old dandelion.

Laying It On Thick

I am Carlos,
painter of eyes and noses,
creator of lips and necks,
maker of the whole figure.
Edmundo is my middle name,
he who manipulates body parts,
the blender of skin and bone,
the only artist west of the Mississippi
who washes his hands in turpentine.
The only painter whose full name
is Carlos Edmundo Frankenstein,
he who makes people come alive with paint,
the only composer of still lifes
that grow out of their frames.

Come to my studio someday.
I have racks full of nudes
and half-dressed fools.
I have portfolios jammed with sketches
of squares and triangles.
So what if I call the triangles *love*
and the squares *hate*?
I am Carlos,
blender of opposites,
Carlos the peacemaker.
Come, take off your clothes
and confess your sins.
If I like what I see, I'll paint you.
If I like what I hear,
I'll frame you.

An Archetype

Inside a square, I draw a circle,
and in the circle, I paint the color green.
Outside the square, I brush in streaks of blue,
and along the bottom of the page
six purple dots.

Meanwhile, inside my body,
a man is painting a yellow rectangle.
He's extending the color beyond
edges, beyond corners.
He lets the paint run.
Now he's making a big black curve
with his brush as if to say, *try;*
you can turn and go back too.

And I do go back, every day,
not to the place where artists paint
but to the geometry of the present,
where the sum of ordinary street corners
equals the angle of unexpected death,
where division among people
coming and going
is multiplied by bloodstains in dark alleys,

where, in a damp and dark subway,
a stranger reaches out
and hugs a circle of dark
and damp air, while a shorter man,
dressed in black, with a derby on his head,
makes a drawing in a sketchbook,
of a tiny man round as a circle,
who lives inside a room perfect as a square.

Family Drawing

It doesn't take much to draw
a line on a piece of paper.
It takes even less
to think of it as a path.
Very little talent is required to draw
a square at one end of the path
and a circle inside the square.
It's easy to call the square *home*,
to know the circle is mother.
It takes a lot of effort to keep
father out of the picture — a big red line
penetrating the circle.

Painting for All Seasons

Eugene paints the sky first,
then the earth below the sky.
He puts some trees in
on the left side,
a pond next to the trees,
a man sitting on a rock
at the edge of the pond,
and a woman lying down
in the buttercups
at the man's feet.
Three sheep graze in the distance,
and on the right side,
a satyr is playing a flute
while a robot does a jig.
In the center of the picture,
Eugene paints a woodpecker nailed
to a cross, with strange birds
flying around. Below the crucified
bird, he renders a big book,
with the pages flapping in the breeze,
a skull in front of the book,
an automobile tire to one side of the skull,
and an old carburetor on top of the skull.
After he signs the picture
in the lower right-hand corner,
he turns the canvas around
and writes the title on the back:
Junkyard Redemption.

Frame Without a Picture

This is the last of the old breath I'm going to take.
And these are the last steps up into the kingdom.
I'm headed for the great territory.
I'm anticipating lyric fields
with lithe grasses bending easily
in the spirit of one holy breeze.
Although I take with me the warts of lust
and the bumps of greed,
although I carry the classic creases
of jealousy, as well as the scars of hate,
all these will pass. Where I'm going,

hate turns into a simple white table;
lust becomes a plain white cup full of wine;
greed changes into a piece of white bread.
And when I drink from the cup,
eat the bread,
jealousy transforms into a white robe
I wear into eternity,
which is so white nobody can describe it,
nor will it ever be painted.
There are no artists in heaven.

REFLECTIONS

'Reflections'   B Boccia

Listening to the Shadows

Years ago when I was made of clay
I looked for pedestals to climb
so that I could pose in the light,
and I believed any book about religion
that said the spirit is the light.
I read about artists who created light
to make shadows. I studied Rembrandt portraits
trying to figure how I could get half of my face
in the dark and the other half in the light.
Every night, at the same street corner,
I'd stand with only half of myself
in the shadow cast by the lamppost.
In my own house I'd crawl between
the lamplight and the wall.
I even managed taking my daily walks
at the time of day when shadows
covered me from my feet to my waist.
I got so good at it I couldn't tell
which I liked best, the light or the dark.
I never felt pain in the parts that were lighted up,
but I did feel as if the shadows were trying
to tell me something —
how if I went deeper into myself,
where it's dark and misty,
I'd come back so bright and shiny
I wouldn't want to pose at all.

The Old Man Gets an Insight

Even though I'm leaning against the toolshed
admiring the magnolia blossoms,
I can't understand what made me
such a believer years ago.
No matter I've got a lily in one hand
and a tulip in the other,
I don't know why I thought shapes and colors
could save my life.
I still think buttercups have something to do with beauty,
but I can't figure what made me see them
blinking up at me, saying,
repent and be free.
Because I was naive,
I'd sit on the back porch for hours
to catch a glimpse of Saint Jerome
peeking out from behind the bushes.
I believed the weather vane was the cock
that crowed three times.
I remember how I raised my right hand
just to bless cocks and saints
and any kind of creature that meant
there was a heaven.

I raise my right hand today,
but it's mostly to shade my eyes.
I lower it mainly to pick up the rake.
I walk real slow too, bent over.
But that's OK. It makes my beard
point so close to a ladybug
crawling between the petunias,
I count her spots.

The Hot and Cold of It

I don't doubt the tulips,
and I never question the roses.
What grows pink dies pink.
What came up green last year
comes up green with yellow in it
this year. No matter the seasons,
artists mix yellow with green
and get summer. With white on white,
they make winter.

Painters turn up the heat
with red-hot color.
They put out bonfires by squeezing
blue all over. Even though Renoir
makes shadows sweat, it's Caravaggio
who makes the darkest shadows curse.

Any man who hides under his bed
at night, cursing the darkness,
ought to buy a Renoir, but any man
who can't stand the sun
should find Caravaggio.

Between Renoir and Caravaggio,
there's always Beckmann, painting
the sun ice-cold blue next to
a red-hot moon.

Frame for All Seasons

The frame takes
the picture
in its arms

the picture
doesn't
move
never does

the head
in the painting
grows old
decays

the canvas
behind the head
rots

someday
the frame will grab
four sides
of space
and it will hug
and hug.

Swallowing Red

Placated by the simple red color
of an unsuspecting apple,
I petition space to make way,
and I say,
He who bites the apple
wounds its color;
he who swallows red
prepares for the life of an artist.

Red on Green

When the motor in the crotch
groans like the old furnace
in the cellar about to burn out
and the whole house smells of smoke,
it's time for me to walk along the path
from the lilacs to the shed
and never once complain about the paint
peeling off the shed door.
It's time for me to keep clear of shadows,
to hold still and turn my head slowly,
the corner of my eye catching a bright-
red spot in the grass — a cardinal
I don't want to scare away.

His Apples Stay in Place

Because his eyes did all the talking,
Cézanne's mouth had nothing to say.
Driven by the shape of things,
he painted shapes round.
Shocked by color, his color shocks
in color waves. He never painted
with his fingers, he never rubbed out.
Red had no edge, not even under blue.
When he divided a pear, the answer was apples.
When he added apples to light, the result
was space. It was the way he focused
on a saucer or a cup. Yes, he flipped
the table up, but that's magic —
his apples and everything else stay in place.
Nothing falls on its face, except us
when we walk away.

Orange Blood

Think of a blue sky
without a touch of yellow.
Imagine magenta
void of the smallest speck
of yellow. Even the sunflower
would hide its face.
Remember being trapped
in a dark room?
Your body gave off light.
That's what yellow does to black.
Now pretend you see
the color yellow itself,
a blob of it.
Think of it spread out
like a field of wheat.
See the sunlight on the wheat?
See the farmer near the barn?
A touch of yellow in his beard
would make him glow.
Even the farmer's daughter
could use a healthy mix
of yellow in her sex life.
It would make things easier
for her boyfriend too.
How wonderful, when the time comes,
to be buried in an earth
that's not inevitably brown
because we remembered to put yellow
into our umber.
So what if it rains in the heart?
I know the heart's red.
But just think what happens
to red when it laps up yellow.
An orange-colored heart
would not only make the blood
move more smoothly than red,
the blood itself would be
pure cadmium orange —
the happiest color to run
through anybody's veins.

After Rolling on My Back

It's gesture I need,
knowing what yellow means
when it's next to green.
I don't want to paint,
not right now.
A little insight while I rest
on my side and more insight
as I roll on my back.
Then a flash:
the ceiling is a sky of cracks;
the stains are yellow angels
without the gain of paradise,
all alone
up there except for the seam
where the beam holds God in place.

Outlived by Seurat

From inside the screen-house,
I look out.
Trees and bushes shoot dots;
pointillism renders the old man
red and yellow spots.
I think of Seurat, or a face
with measles.

The old man never liked art,
didn't trust its dots and dashes.
He took machines for what was real;
his finger on a plug could
heal a spark.
For him, art came in oily splashes, nothing
to do with Picasso's hot flashes.

Outside the screen-house, there are no dots
the eye in focus will not disperse.
The yard paints the shed solid white:
a tomb to put the dead in.
Even the trees know Seurat
will outlive them.

The Artist Knows He Can't Save the World

Right now I'm a ball,
hoping Piero will show up
and draw me as a sphere.

I'm floating upside down,
eager for Chagall to put me
into one of his paintings.

Like a Picasso monkey, I'm swinging
from chandelier to chandelier.
I dive, hit the table,
and smash it into a hundred cubist pieces.

Now I'm kneeling, filling in some of the pieces
with burnt umber and others with yellow.
I'm painting lines in and out of the colors.

Leaning back with my elbows on the floor,
I'm making a circle with my feet.
Pretty soon, the circle will be Cyclops
staring and blinking. I'm flat on my back,

running the heel of my left foot
up and down, making prison bars
not only to prevent the picture
from running wild but to keep the Cyclops
locked in. Later, I'll roll over
on my belly and say a prayer
for every real Cyclops who wants out.

I'll do a *mea culpa* for all the pieces
this world is going to break up into,
and I won't fret about what comes after.
I'll remember that little table,
how it never said, *you broke my legs;*
you cracked my top, how it never tried
to wiggle back into what it was.
I'll remember how it just sat there,
shattered, its parts connected in a new way,
just like us when we sit up in bed
after a bad dream.

Making the Kitchen a Holy Place

When I dress in a white sheet
and fly over the kitchen table,
I look like a cloud with a face.
Although I don't have wings,
I've got a good sense of direction
and a real knack for fooling gravity.
When I land, I do it feetfirst,
in my sneakers.
Last month I lost control
and came down in the sink.
I made such a thump, the little door
of the cabinet flew open, and everything
fell out: the Ivory liquid,
the Comet cleanser, all the Brillo pads and the brush.
Tomorrow, accompanied by cherubim, my three yellow canaries,
and by seraphim, my four lively chickadees,
I'll fly up onto the ceiling,
strike a pose, and hold it without
scratching my nose or rustling my sheet.
My beard may flutter a bit,
but even Michelangelo's prophets
can't control the way the wind blows
on the ceiling of the Vatican.

Half Steps and Two-Steps

After my days as a shovel
and my nights as a pitchfork,
I read Unamuno, which got me into Jung,
who made me look at art.
After spending twenty years posing as an easel
and thirty-five years painting myself up
as a palette, every man wearing a beret
looked like Rembrandt, and every woman
painting a horse resembled Rosa Bonheur,
who could have painted like Picasso
except she wasn't Spanish,
which doesn't matter because nobody
could paint horses like Rosa,
except maybe Piero, and nobody made horses
look like toys better than Ucello,
who was a half step short of cubism,
just like Goya was two steps short
of de Kooning, who painted women and horses
like he'd never run out of paint.

Doing It with the Fingers

It's difficult in these times
to talk to the fence.
It's even harder to hear the fence
talk back. As for lilies, they are deaf.
Thorns pierce. That's why I look for
a simple shaft of light between what was
and what will be, why I'd like to hug
a rose that never bloomed and never will.
Just give me a part of the sky where
the rainbow used to be.
Offer me a tear, and I'll cry too,
but not forever. It doesn't matter
I don't know why I'm here,
why *you* are here. What do we care
the earth is spinning and we're hanging on,
a bunch of fools going nowhere, artists
scratching our heads, poets running
our fingers through our beards?

A Cubist Portrait

Tell me a few jokes
and I'm king.
Pass the meat and the cake
and I'm a rich man.
Sing for me and I don't
hide my face.
Paint my portrait
and I don't sneer.
I know my place:
it's right here,
in this chair,
me, Edward,
with my other self, Eugene,
Edward's face overlapping Eugene's,
Eugene's hands multiplied
by Edward's elbows,
both necks shifting for place,
four shoulders weaving in and out,
fighting for domination —
and all this in one picture.

The Old Man and the Ape

The ape paints like he's never
going to run out of paint.
He throws it on, smears it,
grunts, kicks the easel over
and walks across his painting.
The old man paints in little dabs.
He draws everything first with charcoal,
then carefully goes over the lines
with a small brush and a dark color.
He mixes a few colors, squints, says something
about Michelangelo, steps back,
and falls over the wood stove.
When he gets up, he can't straighten out.
His head hangs and his elbow shakes.

Almost every night the ape and the old man
have a beer and discuss their work.
Tonight, the ape is down on the floor,
looking up, talking into the old man's face.
Meanwhile, the man is trying to make sense
out of the abstractions under the ape's feet.
Why not study anatomy? he asks the grunting ape.
Don't you ever go to the museum?

The Four Loves of Latitia

1

I'm going to marry van Gogh.
Together we'll mix paint
and set up heaps of color.
I'm going to run my fingers
across his face; I'll enjoy
all the crooked planes, the blue lines
around his eyes, and the purple shadow
under his red beard. If he'll let me,
I'll place tiny green eggs in his nest
of bright-orange hair.
I'll let the eggs hatch,
and I'll count the little babies.
It will be easy to straighten out
their feathers. It will be a pleasure
to plop a worm down their throats.

2

I'm going to run away with
Karl Maria Von Weber.
I'll shine his long pointy shoes,
and he'll polish my oval tongue.
I'll abide by his sonatas,
While he unlocks my door.
When I sit back and ask for a kiss,
he'll bend over and write a fugue.
I'd stick my fingers into his lace,
except I'm afraid he'd giggle.

3

Last night I kissed Picasso.
When I turned over, Courbet fell off
my back, and Goya slipped out of my hands.
A yellow light, in the shape of a bulb,
lit up the sky.

4

This morning I pinched Schubert.
He recoiled and offered his silk shirt,
exposed his chest, and said he had always
obeyed the music of his nipples.
I have never been one to hear the flesh sing.
To this day, I believe a song is a force,
an inner force that links death to life.
I take my art where it breathes.

The Tools of the Artist

A saint selects his colors,
a martyr mixes them,
and a sinner does the dirty work
of cleaning his palette.

He remembers the bird feeder
outside his studio window,
how he enjoyed the red color
of the cardinal flicking in and out
of the green leaves,
how the four blue shades of the blue jay
matched the sky after a storm.
Only a flock of crows frightened him,
not because of their color
but because they were so big
they might knock him down.

Better if those birds would tack
his drawings upon his studio wall,
if they would lay out his brushes
and pour the turpentine,
no matter the odor of turpentine
drives the crows crazy
and they pluck his eyes out.
He sees with his heart.

Landscape Without End

When I turn on the stove,
I think of Rome burning.
I think of Nero enjoying the fire
while eating grapes.
I jump centuries ahead and watch
Michelangelo designing the patio
on the Capitoline hill.
Raphael is there, sketching
in the museum of classical sculpture.
And here comes Picasso. He's staring
out of those big, black eyes,
memorizing all those ancient forms
so he can make them his own.
Below the Capitoline,
a small trolley makes its way around a curve
where my good friend John lives. He teaches English
in the American high school on Via Cassia,
the same road Caesar used
to get out of the busy city, to enjoy
the smooth hills and the misty valleys,
the same hills and valleys
Bellini will paint later on,
and even later than that, Corot.

Trouble in the Studio

Come to my studio and see,
but don't get discouraged.
My art is not about angles
or triangles. I don't paint circles;
I never fill in with yellow.
When I render shadows, it means
things are not so good.
When I use light, I use it to blind.

I'm not doing Apollo, I would never
attempt Venus. I'm painting a man
and a woman, all flesh and blood
and alive. The woman's name is Desire;
his name is Lust. Come and see Lust
and Desire hug and kiss. Stay awhile;
it won't be long before she screams
and throws her shoe at him. Don't blink;
you might not see him grab the knife.

In the Park One Day

People came to admire the statue.
Some tried to guess why it shined;
others couldn't figure why
shadows kept moving across it.
An old man in the crowd said the statue
was a work of art.
When they asked him why,
he said someone was inside the statue —
not a person like himself,
or anybody else
but like a creek has a person
because it has a voice,
like a lily has a heart because
it doesn't toil.
When they asked him where he got
such crazy ideas, he didn't answer.
When he pulled his hat
down over his eyes,
somebody threw a beer can at him.

The Artist and the Apes

When apes believed in the Scriptures,
I was home playing hopscotch.
I was only a kid, but already I loved
the white chalk lines on the dark
slate sidewalk, the geometry
of the shapes those lines made.
I had my own language.
And I could write words,
and every word was a picture.
When I added bright colors to the words,
I was talking happy.

After the apes got civilized, they forgot
the Scriptures. I was about sixty then,
painting pictures with lines and shapes.
I told everybody this was my new language.
I explained that when I filled in with yellow,
it meant there's a life after this one,
where everybody is free
and nobody believes in anything.

A Challenge for the Painter

Although I'm not the man who carved the *David*,
I do have a broken nose like Michelangelo.
No matter I didn't paint the *Transfiguration*,
my mistress looks like Raphael's *La Fornarina*.
But I don't paint her — not because she isn't
the baker's daughter but because she burns
with a passion no amount of paint could convey.
I don't even attempt a drawing.
How could my pencil delineate her desire,
my pen do justice to the smoke that comes
from her soul through the crevices of her body?
I defy any painter not only to match
the translucency of that smoke
but to paint her crevices opening and closing,
the way they do when we make love.

Waiting for Perfection

Something wants to come out of the weeds;
something wants to wiggle and be free.
Pindar, the Greek, crawls for his freedom
in a grape. Mr. Caltucci, from La Bella Napoli,
cries for his *sugo al carne.*
Bonnie is dead, and so is Clyde.
Those two never had a real plate of pasta.

Something is trickling — maybe it's history;
maybe it's the faucet.
Something red is dripping.
It could be blood from a wound
or paint through a hole in the floor.

Somebody's husband is putting his shoes
back on. Somebody's wife is taking off her skirt.
My uncle John always wore a stiff white collar.
His neighbor, Pietro Regali Carter, drove
a red convertible. Pietro's cousin Edmund
ate pomegranate after pomegranate,
but he never ate the seeds. I was sixteen,

maybe seventeen, when I planted the seeds
of vindication. By the time I was thirty,
I had planted the five seeds of artistic creation:
When spring came, the plant of *wild dreams*
popped up next to the plant of *never satisfied.*
A week later, I saw the first bud of *technic.*
It looked like a pansy.
Although it wasn't very green,
trial and error had thorns.
Perfection came up last,
but it didn't flower.
Not then.

Better to Drown in Paint

Always the first glow followed
by the second glow.
Always the chatter of the window shade,
the clinking of the bell,
maybe the buoy bell way out at sea,
and there I am on my side, floating
on a raft. Or I'm out there
on the high seas, waving my arms
or rowing in time with the clinking
of the bell.
And what is the bell saying?
Hold on to your oars, old man?
No.
*Work the rudder, let the tide
do the rest?*
No.
It is saying, *better to paint a picture
of a man in a boat lost at sea.
Better to create the low, fast-moving clouds,
to invent the wind and the rain
and the way the man dies.*

Rowing Home

Most of all, I want my model,
and I want her naked like before.
Don't try to carry her. Step aside,
and watch her walk, classical, through my door.
If she should choose to sleep at my feet,
let her be. She not only dreams like a fish,
she talks sleepy undertow. When she turns,
she turns full wave.
But here's a warning: do not stare
at the motion of her hips;
do not listen to her lips.
You could go deaf and blind.
Do what I do: turn the other way,
and paint a seascape blue
as her flesh is green.
Put whitecaps here and there,
to indicate her stormy side.
Now paint yourself in a rowboat
bobbing up and down on her belly.
Do not worry about rowing home —
you have arrived.

THE BLIND ARTIST

the
Blind Artist
E.Boccia

The Blind Artist Doesn't Care About Success

The blind artist sees with the eye
in his belly button. When he mixes color,
the eye blinks.
When he pours turpentine, the eye cries.
Happiness does not enter the eye
in the belly button, and tears come
from the blind eyes of the painter
when the paint drips down
and off the canvas.
Before he even picks up a brush,
the blind artist says a prayer.
Before he puts on his smock,
he throws out all thoughts of success.
Ready for failure, he rubs his fingers
in wet paint, dries them off, burns incense,
and makes the sign of the cross.
The blind artist says his trinity is the easel,
the palette, and the canvas.

Day of Atonement

The blind artist says,
I give you my gift of vision, here;
it has lashes on it
and an old tear.

Blind to emotions, he laughs
when others cry. Sensitive about jokes,
he cries at the first one he hears.

A long line that drips
means a hapless life. A whole bunch of dripping
lines indicates more than one life
is on the brink. No matter drippings
always move downward, no matter
they mess up the floor.
The blind artist waits for the day
when his paint will drip upward.

Tears Below the Belt

Fear motivates the blind artist.
As such, his paintings are dark.
His need for love makes him dizzy.
Therefore his work is blurred.
Pain propels everything he does
and does not do. No wonder
we can't make out his subject matter;
no wonder when we say, *Ah, you have
done another abstraction*, the eye
in the belly button of the blind artist
fills with tears.

A Strain on the Eyes

Be as a child and come into my studio.
By this the blind artist means
we should confess our sins before we visit.
When he insists, *In my studio, be as an infant
in your mother's arms*, he wants us to look
helpless but not stupid.

Although the blind artist honors brains,
he admits too much brainwork makes the eyes pop.

The blind artist believes it's a waste
of time to chase our eyes across the floor
as if they were golf balls.
Art doesn't come, he says, *from the pursuit
of things out there.*

The Big Catch

When he's in his studio, the blind artist
thinks he's at the beach.
When he says, *I slipped on a clam*,
he means he slipped on paint.
When he sweeps his floor clean
of Coke bottles and beer cans,
he thinks it's his brushes sweeping
the sand dunes. He thinks he's sunbathing
when he paints with light.
If he eats his sandwich in the shadow
of his easel, he swears he's eating it
under his beach umbrella.
A cup of coffee on the palette table
is a cup of coffee on his tackle box.

The blind artist believes painting a picture
is like catching a fish: the pigment has to be alive,
like the bait. What he knows has to be sharp
as the hook, and when he hooks the fish,
he doesn't reel it in right away,
just like he never frames his painting
when it's still wet.

Apples on the Floor

Somehow the blind artist knows
the coming of the end of the world
is not his fault. Born to live
in the never-ending world of feelings
and images, the blind artist walks
around with his head high
and his arms stretched out in front.
Born and raised to expect the unacceptable,
the blind artist never recoils.
Favored by the gods who prefer accident
over plan, he never thinks about his next move.
As a follower of the old blind seers,
the blind artist enjoys throwing his model
out of the studio while she is still naked.
He's in ecstasy when he dumps his still life
upon the floor and steps all over it.
When asked how this behavior improves
his creativity, the blind artist says,
there are three things that resemble
the soul — a cool damp place
like an old cellar,
a sweet-smelling woman hungry for love,
and the feeling we get when we eat raw meat.

Down to the Bone

The blind artist likes to visualize
himself dead in his casket.
To see himself laid out makes the blind artist
realize there's no sense painting for money or fame.

Since painting is all about nothing,
the blind artist never counts his pictures.
Every time he finishes one,
he puts it away in his cellar.

Because he thinks his cellar is the catacombs,
the blind artist has no doubt his pictures
will die and leave their bones.

Although the cellar of the blind artist
is in St. Louis and not in Rome,
he does expect some tourists.

A Little Something for Everybody

Born into this world to enlighten
the living who are dead in spirit,
the blind artist makes drawings
of ghosts in white sheets.
Born for those who are alive in spirit
but dead in body, he draws
funeral homes with big porches.
When the blind artist sketches
the town morgue to look like
the Taj Mahal, he's preparing a place
for those who believe in the afterlife.

One for the Road

The blind artist paints like a driver
who's had one too many.
He makes turns with his brush
like an old man turns the steering wheel of his Ford.
Every lump of paint on the palette
is a concrete bump on the road.
The blind artist would like to avoid
holes between his images,
but he doesn't see them coming.
Hoping to paint straight,
he makes U-turns.
He screams when he comes to a dead end.
The blind artist has had it with red lights
and yellow flashes.

Travel leaves its scars. Just going
from one end of his canvas to the other
requires all the blood the blind artist can pump up.
He'd drink gasoline if he thought
it would keep him painting longer.
He'd oil his feet
if it would make the trip smoother.

To Him It Comes Easy

The blind artist sees through everybody and everything.
When his brother hid from him in the coal bin,
the blind artist saw right through the coals.
When his cousin Evelyn ran away,
he got there before she did.

The blind artist not only paints in his studio
and in his head at the same time,
he draws in his dreams while he's awake.

We struggle for a little light in our world,
while he paints with light.
We fight for our freedom, and he breaks all the rules.
We need to build bridges, and he paints rainbows.

We make a toast to Titian, and the blind artist
refuses to join in. When we say, *Ah, here's to you
and only you*, he not only raises his glass,
he gulps the wine down and spills half of it
in his beard.

The Blind Artist as Actor

The blind artist draws a circle inside a square.
After he draws another square inside the circle,
he tacks the drawing up, sits back, and calls it
the eye in the eye of the world.
When the blind artist fills in a shape with red paint,
he's offering his own blood for the good of art.
When he paints green all around the red shape,
he's surrounding the act of sacrifice.
When he feels hopeless, the blind artist
smears black paint in broad strokes across his canvas.
When he feels like crying, he grabs his paint rag
and blows his nose. When the tears come,
he lets them fall on his palette.
Although he realizes oil and water don't mix,
he never gives up trying.
It's not unusual to see the blind artist roll
across his studio floor in a fit of passion.
It's not unusual to see him roll across the floor
just for the fun of it. Because he's a superb actor,
it's hard to tell which is which.

Gifts from the Sea

In the name of freedom,
the blind artist looks
at a green apple
and paints it purple.
In the name of idea,
he renders a man's head
like a sphere.
To get that spiritual quality,
he mixes yellow with pink.
After he makes light,
the blind artist sees shadows.
Since he can't see the dark
night of the soul, he paints
his canvas black, and hangs it
in the light.

The blind artist says thick paint
stands for struggle
and thin paint means this is
a liquid world and we all
ought to get into our psychological
boats and go with the tide.
Because he hates the sand dunes
of frustration, the blind artist
paints the high tide of success
till it runs over the beaches
of tranquillity.

If it's peace he wants, he dabs
a small white cloud on a flat
blue sky. Two gray clouds and
a streak of black means things
are about to become overcast.
When he paints snakes twisting
above the horizon, it's a sure sign
the nor'easter of hate is about
to wreck the boardwalk of love.
But before it does, the blind artist
puts his brushes down, runs
upstairs and hides under his bed.

The Blind Artist Helps His Audience

Every time the blind artist says he moves
the still life, he's talking about
moving an apple from here to there.
When he moves an apple or an orange
from here to there, the blind artist
knows he's moving the only life he's got.

Although the blind artist is able
to figure the difference between
being alive and things moving,
he can't get it clear what part
of himself stays put after he makes a move.

Blind to appearances, he confuses intent
with pain. The blind artist feels he'd
get a handle on himself if he knew more
about who he isn't.

Since the object of art, for the blind artist,
is to paint what isn't seen,
he puts a lot of stock in making mistakes
look good. When the blind artist makes
a small mistake, like painting a red rose
yellow, he makes it look good by putting
a little green into the yellow.

A bigger mistake, like painting a man's head
on a woman's body, gets to look OK
when he puts a cigar in the man's mouth.

The biggest mistake of all, such as painting
the sea upside down, is corrected as soon as
the painter turns the canvas upside down.

Upside down or right side up, it's a good thing
the blind artist writes the date on the back.
It's better than good when he signs it.
The best part is the title: how else
would we know what the painting means?

Biographical Note

Edward Boccia was born in Newark, New Jersey, in 1921. After graduating the Pratt Institute, he entered World War II as a camouflage engineer in Europe. He had his first one-man show in the Intimate Gallery at Pratt in 1945. He received his B.S. and M.A. degrees from Columbia University. In 1958, he was awarded the Borsa di Studio from the Italian government for study in Italy. He has lived in that country with his wife and children off and on for twenty-five years. He was knighted to the Cavaliere al Merito della Republica by the president of Italy in 1979.

From 1951 to 1986, Boccia was Professor of Fine Arts in the School of Fine Arts at Washington University, St. Louis. His work is part of many public and private collections in the U.S. and Europe. In 1990, St. Louis University, home to some one hundred Boccia paintings, made him a member of the Order of the Crown of King St. Louis IX.

Boccia began writing poetry in 1980. His chapbook *Moving the Still Life* was published by Pudding House in 1993. He has received over forty awards, with prizes from the Wednesday Club of St. Louis, the World Order of Narrative Poets, *Negative Capability*, *Blue Unicorn*, and *Rhino*, and his poems have appeared in numerous publications, including *California Quarterly*, *The Eliot Review*, *CSS Publications*, *Orbis*, *Live Poets Society*, *Atlantic Review*, and *Poetpourri*.

Also available from Time Being Books

LOUIS DANIEL BRODSKY
You Can't Go Back, Exactly
The Thorough Earth
Four and Twenty Blackbirds Soaring
Mississippi Vistas: Volume One of *A Mississippi Trilogy*
Falling from Heaven: Holocaust Poems of a Jew and a Gentile
  (with William Heyen)
Forever, for Now: Poems for a Later Love
Mistress Mississippi: Volume Three of *A Mississippi Trilogy*
A Gleam in the Eye: Poems for a First Baby
Gestapo Crows: Holocaust Poems
The Capital Café: Poems of Redneck, U.S.A.
Disappearing in Mississippi Latitudes: Volume Two of *A Mississippi Trilogy*
Paper-Whites for Lady Jane: Poems of a Midlife Love Affair
The Complete Poems of Louis Daniel Brodsky: Volume One, 1963–1967
Three Early Books of Poems by Louis Daniel Brodsky, 1967–1969: *The Easy Philosopher*, *"A Hard Coming of It" and Other Poems*, and *The Foul Rag-and-Bone Shop*

HARRY JAMES CARGAS (editor)
Telling the Tale: A Tribute to Elie Wiesel on the Occasion of His 65th Birthday — Essays, Reflections, and Poems

JUDITH CHALMER
Out of History's Junk Jar: Poems of a Mixed Inheritance

GERALD EARLY
How the War in the Streets Is Won: Poems on the Quest of Love and Faith

ALBERT GOLDBARTH
A Lineage of Ragpickers, Songpluckers, Elegiasts & Jewelers: Selected Poems of Jewish Family Life, 1973–1995

ROBERT HAMBLIN
From the Ground Up: Poems of One Southerner's Passage to Adulthood

WILLIAM HEYEN
Erika: Poems of the Holocaust
Falling from Heaven: Holocaust Poems of a Jew and a Gentile
  (with Louis Daniel Brodsky)
Pterodactyl Rose: Poems of Ecology
Ribbons: The Gulf War — A Poem
The Host: Selected Poems, 1965–1990

TED HIRSCHFIELD
German Requiem: Poems of the War and the Atonement of a Third Reich Child

VIRGINIA V. JAMES HLAVSA
Waking October Leaves: Reanimations by a Small-Town Girl

RODGER KAMENETZ
The Missing Jew: New and Selected Poems
Stuck: Poems Midlife

NORBERT KRAPF
Somewhere in Southern Indiana: Poems of Midwestern Origins
Blue-Eyed Grass: Poems of Germany

ADRIAN C. LOUIS
Blood Thirsty Savages

GARDNER McFALL
The Pilot's Daughter

JOSEPH MEREDITH
Hunter's Moon: Poems from Boyhood to Manhood

BEN MILDER
The Good Book Says . . . : Light Verse to Illuminate the Old Testament

TIME BEING BOOKS
POETRY IN SIGHT AND SOUND

FOR OUR FREE CATALOG OR TO ORDER
(800) 331-6605 · FAX: (888) 301-9121
http://www.timebeing.com